Белой Горячки

Галлюцинации очень
возможны.

Brain Fever #2

Publisher
Gene Yu

Editor
Mike Goodman

Produced quarterly by
Matchlock Press
PO Box 90606
Brooklyn, NY 11209

Correspondence
Write to us c/o Matchlock Press, or
email brainfever@matchlock.com.

Contents

EDITORIAL

Hello! Greetings to you! I'm sending out a hug & a kiss & a little pinch on your pretty derriere! Whoever you are & whatever is the state of that derriere you're carrying around!

Feelings being what they are in the land, why don't you take your head out of the oven for a minute, anyway? What harm could it do you? It'll still fit in a couple of hours. Log off & get out of the house for a minute. See some old friends (friends you can stand, not those fuckers, quislings, and shit-eating racists)! Do what you can to put your heart back together. Or at least pick up that smashed old girl and put the pieces in your pocket. We're going to try & find you some glue! Just a dab, dab here, a dab, dab there. You're doing better already! A story about an idiot friend of mine & Vietnam, some comix fresh from space, more from a rich white lady who can't get along with her daughter, & a couple of new features: Sharp Cards, a strip about a bug. See if you like it!

We've got to wake up to the future. Not big philosophy, just what we all know. That's why we're hurting here. We're stuck in some kind of time bubble where we can't move on. But let's shake off the fear and pain! Heavy! Heavy, they used to say, in all senses of the thing. The long road, the steps backward, the enemies. The feeling of awe all around. Because the enemy is formidable, and sometimes we feel like we're looking up at it all, just like ants. But bless you ants! *Formicae* with your giant crumbs—50× your own small weight—carried manfully on your backs.

So, Love!

Get in the fight!

Peace in the streets!

Formulate your truth, and live in there!

Kiss your neighbor!

Take on the old and young! Make them yours! Cook them some fucking soup! Good soup, not from a BPA-riddled can!

Love your Earth more! Do what you can to hold onto her! Put your cheek to her beautiful green breast and hear her heart beat. Everyday, if you can!

See the blessing that is this given day, given to you for courage, meaning, purpose!

I love you!   Mike

A REMINISCENCE

BY

MIKE GOODMAN

GLOBAL warming has shot the seasons to shit in the North Country. Did you hear they started tapping the maple trees a month early this year? But the majority of the time, it's still cold as damn hell upstate in the winter. You have to have the gear: lined pants, glove warmers (shit for the environment, possibly made with excess napalm, but worth it for your hands), good waterproof boots from some company in Maine, hat with earflaps, long underwear, and something on your hands. All that time it takes you to suit up for battle, at the end of it you can't even find a reason to go outside. Modern dogs are independent; they let themselves back in and out, and some of you disposable-income burghers have the heated garage attached to the house. Even if it's only for the two-minute walk from the parking lot to the store, though, I always keep in mind that picture of the car breaking down, and gear up accordingly. You don't want to set out on a hike back towards town to get some cell reception with a pair of driving moccasins on. You won't keep your feet very long!

If you're not an outdoorsman, you might not be aware that anything's going on outside at all. As remedy, try some snowshoeing. Go deeper into the woods and look for the rabbit tracks, deer tracks. Everything back there is undisturbed and quiet. Go at dawn or dusk for that blue light on the snow. Maureen has tried to paint it on several occasions but her watercolors froze. Her ass froze, too, sitting out there.

If you're too much of a coward to head outside, you have to turn to the twin pillars of modern American society: television and Walmart. Fifteen hours later you emerge from that place with three hundred dollars worth of lube, sport socks, and an imitation Timex on your wrist, none of which you need! You bought it just on the off chance you get someone to ball, or a sport, or finally get a job and need to get to work on time! That's the vampire Walmart, sucking up your time and money!

If you live in a cold climate, you better be a reader or have a serious hobby. I don't know how you're going to make it without that. I hear the Icelanders spend the whole national GNP on books at Christmas time. Probably it's less now, as the US is big on exporting stupidity all around the world. In the US, intellectual deterioration has picked up pace over the last fifteen years. We were dumb enough before; it's hard to imagine we could get worse, but you'll see what I mean if you go outside and have a conversation with some people.

I've been saying for years it's caused by the lack of hobbies. Where is the American hobby now? Caning, working on cars. Fucking scrimshaw! Quilting, fly-tying, marquetry, soapbox cars, cross-stitch, ham radio, playing fiddle, beading, chemistry sets in the garage. That's what made America great. These elaborate hobbies that took thought and time to learn. You think the president has a hobby? The Goldman fucking Sachs execs he hired? They think a hobby is for lazy shits with too much time on their hands. (But they also think foreplay is for weaklings who can't get what they want any other way. You almost could feel sorry for them if you realize all the things they're missing out on.) We're slamming against the ass end of the American experiment. The hobbyists are how we got to the moon, you dumb fuckers! People with imagination, curiosity. Satanists with kettle drums of rocket fuel in the garage behind their houses.

Maureen will now point out to you that by February, I too head out to participate in rural America's other national pastime, and go shopping at Walmart. That's factual, but somehow misses the nuance. I go, but only under extreme protest. Have you ever subjected yourself to those lights? And we'll hang out in the library for a few hours afterward to get the stink out. You have to take a pass through Althusser and smoke a joint immediately after in the parking lot. Do something to bring back those brain cells you just killed.

This has been titled "Indian Bingo," not "Fuck the Walmart Family," so let's move on to my point here. Maybe we'll slide in my magnum opus "Fuck the Walmart Family" next issue if we have room: "A raw story, of untenable beauty," says Kirkus Reviews.

Here's the present story, though: I had a friend—let's call him John, as John was his name and that's cover enough since half of the people in the story are named John—and he did not want to go to Vietnam. Nobody wanted to go to Vietnam, I assure you, but unlike everybody else with a conscience in North America, John did not have a moral problem with the war, a fear for his life, or even a stand on killing per se, and he didn't have an opinion or a care as to whether or not the people in the North should be Communists, whether they were innocent victims or perpetrators, or anything else about it. If you had shown him a picture of Hitler and his sainted grandmother side by side, he would be hard-pressed to say which one he preferred, both being people. A bizarre way of looking at things, John had.

John grew up a hunter, and I personally had seen him take out a ten-point buck with no compunction about bringing down such a monumental beast—a mammal with its own life behind the eyes, its own loves, moving through the forest with purpose and authority—for no real reason at all, and not because he liked to eat venison. He said it was too gamey. I'm sure he gave all the meat away.

He was bloodthirsty and he didn't even bother to conceal it. He would get up close to the dead animal and take pictures for his scrapbook. A disgusting guy in a lot of ways. Calling him my friend is taking it too far. Looking back it's a wonder anyone else liked him either, but they seemed to, and eventually he even got a nice lady who let him stick it in her. There are the kids to prove it happened. No sense in the world!

As I pointed out, John's attitude about the war aligned with the rest of the civilized world by coincidence only. But his attitude caused him as much trouble as if he had beliefs and a moral compass. He hadn't gone to

college and had no other outs in the offing. John had no reasonable dodge for avoiding service either. Not in school, no kid and wife. Privately, we all knew he hadn't yet gotten to second base with a girl. Everyone teased him about that, but it didn't raise a blush on his pimply cheeks. He acted like it was a badge of honor and a sign of his elevated æsthetics. (Of which he had none. You'd know if you'd have seen his apartment or the clothes he wore. Colorblind, too, if I recall.)

"I'm waiting for the right pair of tits," he would say, and guffaw. "Hah, hah, hah." Not an appealing laugh either. "Tell us about the tits, John! The dream tits!" and that dude would wax on! There's a lot to say about tits, but not as much as this guy drummed up. He was some kind of savant. Could write the purest encomiums, but on one topic only. Mind you, he'd never seen a pair in the flesh. Not even his mother's, he told us so. Just from girlie magazines. I'm not sure if he could even say whether tits should be hard or soft. There was some confusion about it, when you pressed him.

That was about the caliber of the conversation with that group. College was a breath of fucking fresh air after that. You have no idea how I dug those conversations once I got there. The Jewish frat brothers, maybe four of the pledges, were in my intro philosophy class first semester, and we would go down to this shit bar in town, Gurneys, and drink pitchers and talk about those old Germans, those cats like Kant and Heidegger. Bringing them up with our dads, they might have stroked out, which made it all the better. My dad never bought a German product, never read a book by a German unless the author was Jewish, too. He didn't read that much in general, truth be known.

The bar had a grill where the grease was about a palm thick on the walls. The cook was always sitting out back on an overturned can of cooking oil smoking a cigarillo. They never had a bar of soap in the bathroom, and in those days they didn't wear gloves when dealing with raw meat. But it was a treat to eat that poisonous shit he cooked. Somehow it even sat well, as unlikely as it sounds.

Freshman year, coming home for Thanksgiving, I met up with my old group of friends again. Already feeling like a superior bastard, three months in. It doesn't take long to set in, but it takes a hell of a long time to wear off afterwards. We went to a bar in town. The drinking age was eighteen then, for you kids who are wondering about it. (I'm still not sure how they expect college kids to make it through four years completely sober. That's never made any sense to me.) Of course the draft came up almost immediately. John had gotten a low number, really low. Like he was next up, next time the draft board shuffled the papers on their desk. It was a shame for him, and we all shook our heads in sympathy, but John did not sound bummed out at all.

"Not worried about it, gentlemen," he said. "I'm not planning on going." No? It was a pretty bald-faced pronouncement, and John cheerfully told us he had an uncle in Canada who would put him up and employ him. "Not because I'm a coward," he assured us. "I'm sure even you men could vouch for me under oath. I've never backed away from a fight, have I?" Us assembled guys looked at each other. John was the type you couldn't take anywhere when he got really drunk because he'd start walking up to people and picking fights. Again, I stress it: a real asshole. "Not fear. Not cowardice. It's because I live in this body, and I know it better than anyone else. And it's taken this whole time to figure out how it runs, and how to make it run to perfection. I can't let some sergeant fuck it up. I've got to run it, and I've got to run it my way." Looking at that kid—he had this clownish look on his face, really serious, like he was dropping science on the group of us—there was not a dry eye in the house. Someone taking a sip of beer even sprayed some down his shirt front, we were laughing so hard.

"I can't be in a situation where I don't control where and when I take a shit. I cannot be someplace with no shitter at the end of the day." We just could not stop laughing at this. It was true: The times we went hunting together, he'd complained the whole day about having to take a shit. He never stopped talking about how he had to hold it, and what it was doing to his bowels, what it would be like to take that shit later when it was all clogged up in there. It was his only topic of conversation.

"And I won't eat food out of packets. I won't do it. That's not food." John came from a family where even his grandfather cooked pretty well, cowboy style. John himself was a bachelor living in a crappy eighteen-year-old's apartment over a garage, and still had not figured out how to do his laundry. His place stank, but he cooked himself beef stew for one, and potatoes au gratin on a hot plate. This was like a magic act to the rest of us, the idea that the ingredients would all fuse into something new. We never paid attention to what our moms were doing in the kitchen. Myself, I had foregone the meal plan to save money for books and beer, and ended up eating Cheerios with tuna fish every night for pretty much the whole four years. I wasn't even the only guy I knew who did it. That was the gourmet poverty. A concept was actually behind it. The food

in Vietnam would have been an improvement over what I was eating, even if it was all out of packets. A pickle and a container of salt would have made it Le Cirque.

But not so for John. He was a full-out foodie for the times! Maybe less kale and fermented items than the cats eat now, of course!

"And I have to shower every day, and twice a day in summer. If I don't, athlete's foot. Heat rash. This kind of crinkly feeling on my neck. And God help my balls!" He cradled them in some seriousness. Everyone was laughing their asses off hearing John characterize his woes. He was like a fucking old man.

"Anything else?" the other John asked. "You have some requirement for Ben Gay, or a glass you put your teeth in?" John ignored him and continued on piously.

"Yes. I need a full night's sleep. Every night. No exceptions. I'm not like the rest of you, here and there snatching what you can get. I have to brush my teeth, wash my face, jerk off, and be done by 9:30. And if I don't get to bed by then, I have to wake up that amount later, you get it? Whatever it is, it has to add up to ten full hours. No exceptions." Jesus Christ, we roared at this. That little ugly prick sociopath telling us about his old-maid sleeping habits like he was some kind of beautiful orchid that needed to be misted five times a day. The kid stank for someone who claimed to wash his face so much.

There is a certain kind of teenager who goes through a puritanical stage like this, looking down on everyone else, before breaking out into chaos and rebellion. And there's something sweet about that, looking back, even though at the time they're always really superior about their trip. Really, they're trying hard to hold on to their childhoods just a little longer. But these claims were something else! Something fucking else!

Everyone wants their body taken care of, to be in a state of comfort. Even animals are smart enough to figure that out, and John was acting like he had some kind of great revelation. Some kind of sophisticated philosophical understanding the rest of us could barely get. But this stuff's not the central issue when you're choosing to go to war. Most people get that right off. They're worried about holding on to their lives, trying not to die before they've even gotten laid, and that's the selfish part of it. The other part is killing. Those things are usually what bother people most, if you can tolerate me stating the obvious for a few. But you're a sharp cat; none of this was obvious to John.

"You're going to bug out forever over where you take a shit? What are you saying? If they had flush toilets in Vietnam, you'd sign up?"

"Yes, sir, motherfucker! I would serve if I knew they would supply me with my comforts. Damn skippy! You want your feet falling off the bone, have at it. Those fuckers get trench foot, and they can never wear regular shoes again. I don't have a problem with dragging the guts out of a VC, though. You've got to do that if you want the leather." Jesus fuck! I'll remember that comment forever. On my deathbed I'm going to bring all of my family in close, my grandkids by then I hope, and in a hoarse and almost indistinguishable voice I'm going to croak out, "You . . . know . . . what . . . that . . . motherfuck . . . John . . . said . . . about . . . the . . . VC? . . . And . . . my . . . fucking . . . mother . . . loved . . . him. . . ." Then immediately I'll knock off. Once it's out I can take my leave. That utterance from that son-of-a-bitch is why they spat on the soldiers when they came home. And look! The only fucker saying things like that didn't even serve.

Everyone who'd seen John take down the buck, or one like it, was not surprised by anything he said. I'm not calling all hunters human-killers, you know, but they've certainly got a head start on it over the rest of us. And John was sprinting pretty far up past the pack.

No one doubted he meant not to go, but between meaning it and actually lamming it, there's usually some gulf. I've said a lot of things I've meant over the years that I haven't gotten close to doing. As have we all, I'd like to think. I'd list mine for you, but then I'd have to go hang myself. This plan of his turned out to be serious, and a few months later, over mid-winter break, I got a letter from my mother detailing all of the local gossip, with special emphasis on my old classmate John. John's mother reported generally and at large to all the women who would listen (which was all of them, of course, for they were rabid for news of us the more we seemed to slip their clutches) that John had gotten called into his induction center, and fled to Canada rather than be drafted. No effort at all, it seemed, to claim that he liked to take it up the ass, or was wigged out on drugs (and of course my mother mentioned none of that). No effort or preparation into it, just took off under cover of night, as they say, but probably just around noon as if he were taking a very pretty Sunday drive to see the falling snow. Whatever the manner by which he went, that cat was gone. Forwarding address not to be passed on; unknown for all intents and purposes.

While John's mother was talking all over town about it, John's father, who was somewhat more normal than his son, was embarrassed as hell that John had taken off. Like all of our fathers, John's had served, and the story went that John's father was too embarrassed to even go into the VFW

anymore and have a beer after his son left town. It's probably even true that the other men blamed him for raising what might, in some regional argot, be called a pussy. I wouldn't know. Even at that early point, I was on my way to becoming a full-fledged long-hair, and wasn't asking around in that set for anyone's opinion on the state of his son's masculinity. "Hey man, Mr. Stewart, I've got an important question here for you for an opinion piece I'm putting together. Would you say I'm more or less of a faggot than your son John, since I look like a girl, but he's a draft dodger? Feel free to take your time with that answer. I realize you're an expert, and there's a lot of nuance to cover."

My mother, who was a left-leaner and never would tell my father whom she voted for, tried to convince John's mother, who was pretty much hysterical for a time, that John was acting with his conscience, and that he was doing the right thing because of it. My mother was always trying to get people to do right, think right. I hated this about her for a long time. There was something snippy and prudish about it. Beneath her, I thought. Like someone at the church bake sale peering critically at everyone else's apple crumble.

Hearing this whole fucking tale from my mother made it seem like John was some sort of Quaker, down on his knees taking the bayonet peacefully, with his eyes on God. He was a terrible person. I couldn't seem to explain it to her at all. Much as I was happy, then as now, to see people resisting, I tried to set my mother straight in my return letter without actually including the truth of the problem. This was the way things seemed to work back then, in my life at least. Your whole life back then was a fucking write-around. Trying to get some information across without actually naming it. (The letter she kept nicely in a box labeled "Mike's Correspondence—College and Grad School." Even thirty years later, she was still pointing out that the box never got halfway full. Those clean letters didn't let out half of what was going on with me. There are letters somewhere, if God keeps intentions stored and stocked, and they would have filled that box. Letters crammed with lovemaking, LSD, pyres stacked high with bullshit and lit by spit and matches, and all kinds of things that my mother did not want to hear about and that I did not want to tell her about.)

But I tried to tell it to her in terms that she could work with: "John is not a political person! He doesn't know or understand anything about this war. He couldn't define Communism for you. Clearly he's got a complex, Mother. Do you know what that is? In my opinion, he's a classic anal-retentive." That last bit still makes me laugh! You can tell what class I was taking that semester!

Looking back over the letter, I can still feel the emotions that were be-

hind it. And there was something else, too, that you might not be able to catch there: I was jealous of the balls he had. And his confidence, even if what he directed that confidence at was stupid. I don't think I had any courage at all at that age. I was always slinking out of places when it looked like someone might start swinging, and it really pissed me off that my mother or anyone else might think well of him. You'd think I would have supported any reason a kid came up with to dodge. The person I was then doesn't even make sense to me now.

As far as what was passed on to me that year through the local grapevine— and my mother made sure to tend her stretch of that grapevine quite well— John ended up doing fine living in Canada under an assumed name, and working off the books for his uncle. John found a girlfriend, and didn't miss the US at all. From the evidence, he seemed to be doing much better in Canada than he had done while still at home.

If you could read between the lines, some of his control freak tendencies, which had driven him up there in the first place, seemed to have worn off. By spring semester that year, his mother reported to my mother that he and his girlfriend were taking regular weekend camping trips, which meant that somehow he had found a way to take a shit in the woods, God bless him. Or he just held it for a day or two, and dealt with the consequences later when his girlfriend wasn't around. But there's only so much time I want to devote to an exploration of John's improved bowel health, if you'll excuse me.

In their reported discussions, those mothers took no interest in John's neurotic troubles, and seemed to forget that he was a fugitive on the run. The talk between them centered entirely now on John's unmarried status, and the sleepovers he was likely having with the girlfriend, so far away from American civilization in the wilds of Canada. It seemed to the collected housewives that the mores were different up there,

and John was rapidly falling prey to a sloppy and dissolute morality, the type that might make girls toss out their panty girdles and everyone stop their compulsive ironing. From that to dildos and polyamorous triads was a hop, skip and a jump, and those women sensed it on the wind!

My mother reported: "Mrs. X tells me the girl lives on her own and is a few years older than John. To anyone's knowledge, they are not even engaged. Certainly he has not mentioned it to his mother."

Most flatteringly, now that I look at it, though at the time the misunderstanding really pissed me off, my mother concluded that letter with the following: "Michael, just because you are far enough from home that your father and I can't see what you are doing, don't forget the values that we and the rabbi have tried to convey to you. Remember, Michael, that girls have mothers and fathers, too, and those mothers and fathers want to think that their daughters are with boys they can trust, boys who have the girls' best interests at heart!" Looking over it now, she underlined that last bit with another color of pen, that's how important the topic was to her! But this was the time when you had to be a married woman to get a prescription for The Pill. It was the dark ages all around.

I was nowhere near a girl my freshman year of college. At the time it caused me a lot of pain to hear that John was on track to lose his virginity, and it caused me even more confusion that such a dud like him could find a girlfriend when I was alone every weekend with no one but unwilling set-ups to take to the fraternity dances. My sexuality was limited to afternoons when my roommate was out at marching band rehearsal, jerking it like it was a hateful but necessary medical procedure. A sad chapter!

The story of John and his self-exile thickened before it thinned again. I heard some of these details from my mother, and some of it at our twentieth reunion from the horse's mouth. "What the hell ever happened to get you into the jam you were in, John? How did it go so wrong?" We just swarmed him at the table, rudely ignoring our wives, and commandeering a bottle of that shit Crown 7 from the open bar. We made him tell us the whole tale, which was for the best, because the Creedance Clearwater Revival cover band they hired for the reunion was making me want to take my life, anyway. "Why the fuck didn't it work out with Canada? And what about that girlfriend of yours up there? The older one?" He was kind of amazed that we all knew so much of the story, and of course his ego was tickled, as the mothers in our town had made him famous, at least in the tiny circles they went in.

John gave us the full report. Honestly, I've slagged him a lot but he grew up to be a laid back guy, and not much like who he was. I can share a joint with

him from time to time and reminisce, though I'm not going to scratch the surface too deeply and find out what's going on beneath. Suffice it to say, I'm not inviting him over to the house when my daughter's visiting, or going out to the woods with him. I don't hunt anyway, and haven't after the first moment I found the power to bow out of it.

So here's how John's story turned out the way it did. John had a great deal of sang froid when it came to fleeing. He got the fuck out of dodge with focus and military precision, and it seemed no one but his mother was the wiser as to where he had gone. But John had two weaknesses when it came to America, and these two kept drawing him back over the border when he should have just stayed put.

First off, he missed his mother, an idea I wouldn't have understood at all at the time, but which I'm now all too familiar with. They had some kind of intense relationship, those two, the kind where you confide your worries and all that. The second weakness is even harder to fathom than the first, which is also pretty hard to fathom. Apparently, as a young man of eighteen, he had a thing for Indian Bingo. No other form of gambling could fill the bill: craps or keno or playing poker like the rest of us. (John didn't really have the mind for poker. In high school, he was always asking one of us to remind him about the rules in the middle of a hand. Back then we always said it was like asking a girl to join the game. "Don't play poker in a house with women," you know, and all that. Yeah, it's fucked up, I know, but I'm always frank with you about my lapses. No point in getting mad about it now forty, fifty years on. Still, I don't know that many women who like to play, or remember the rules well when they do. Yet I'm not saying anything about that. Most just find it boring, I think. And Maureen can kill me in any battle of memory. All sensible men know

women are smarter in head and heart!) Not a week without Indian Bingo, or else he would languish! I find bingo a real downer myself, whether it involves money or not—at least when you're doing regular gambling it's an excuse to have a few drinks, but this gambling he was doing was dry! I'll take his world for it; to this day he still talks about it like he's planning on getting laid with some favorite lady after a very long dry spell. Indian Bingo!

Once a week John would slip back into the US and meet his mother at the Mohawk Reservation up near the border. He and his mother would play bingo, talk together about whatever it was. Probably she cried a little, and berated him about making it with his girlfriend before even putting a ring on her finger. Then she would send him off with several shopping bags filled with food: a roast turkey sideways in the bag, homemade rolls, something done up with sweet potatoes. Maybe a Bundt cake, as well. Enough to last him through the week, though John was a very good cook himself and would have done fine without it, and despite the fact that he now had a girlfriend with whom he was clearly keeping house, if you weren't blind to the signs. "She was the best cook in the family," he said later about his mother. "Hands down."

For the most part, John told me, he was cautious about where he crossed back and forth. Never took the most direct route. Went out of his way quite a bit to find the best roads. At the time that border was what they call porous pretty much up and down. Everyone other than big-rig truckers could find a dirt road to rattle down, unnoticed. There were a few routes to take that people knew then, and generally John switched it up and was pretty careful.

Sometimes, he reported, there was even some doubling back.

That's to say he was cautious for the first year or so, and then he forgot all about the fact that he was a fugitive from justice and began driving on the highway whenever he could get away with it, and not even driving slow. He would speed on the highway. Freshman-year Mike—that weedy fucker—who has just returned from picking blackheads in the communal bathroom to show you his Psych midterm, C+ and a couple of snarky comments from the Professor in red on top, is going to tell you that John was working off some kind of subconscious guilt complex and he wanted to get caught. As I said, John's father was a veteran and had served with dis-

tinction. What I know of John now, and hearing him talk about it as a man decades removed, I think he genuinely forgot himself. He was riding easy with his girl and his new job up there, and didn't even seem to remember why he'd gone in the first place.

So of course, inevitable to our story—how else did you think it would turn out?—one day in the frigid winter of my sophomore year, a cop pulled him over on the American side of the border. He was going ninety-five and had only one driver's license to offer, which was his American license with his own fugitive name on it and his own ugly fugitive mug beside it. What sort of fugitive doesn't even get himself fake ID? Even cheap fake ID? He was far enough from home, and from anyone who knew him, that the cop gave him his ticket, and looking at his nice white face and short haircut, sent him on his way. Didn't call it in, or do anything about it at all. Black boy up to the same thing would have been pulled out of his car and never found his way back to it. Same thing then as now, with almost no change at all in the intervening years!

Options John had: Lay low and forget about the ticket. No new repercussions at all except for missing his mother and Indian Bingo for several months. No need to pay it, since it would hardly have added much to the crimes on his shoulders.   Or: Pay his ticket through his mother and also lay low. Again, no repercussions at all except for missing his mother and Indian Bingo for several months. Or he could keep doing exactly what he was doing, the plan of action that seemed destined to work out so well for him. But as all his friends said later, John had always been a bit of an idiot, and he continued to be one. If one out of the three options was the stupid one to take, that was the one that appealed to John.

Instead of doing the sensible thing—any sensible thing!—he gave not another thought to any of it, and returned the next week for his standing date with his mother. That in itself was enough to qualify him as a real fucking idiot, but that wasn't the end of it. Again he drove ninety-five on that fucking highway, and for a second time he was pulled over. Pulled over by the same cop! As you might imagine, the cop had gotten in trouble for not calling it in when it turned out that John was a known draft dodger, using his own license! Not being as stupid as John, though funnily enough that cop's name was John, too, that guy had no intention of making the same mistake twice.   Even a full-blooded peacenik would have hauled in a kid like this, stupid enough to pull the same stunt twice in close succession. Fate was just coming to John, and he was walking right towards it.

John served fifteen months for draft evasion in a jail cell that he claimed, over beers, was right next door to Muhammad Ali. When he told the story, no one had the heart to point out that unlike John, Ali never actually served time in jail for the crime. Ali was an actual conscientious objector who had a moral and religious problem with the war, whereas my friend John's only real objection was about where he might be able to take a shit. ℮

Eds. Note: Sorry, no balling! I had bad acne and low self-esteem freshman year, and was absolutely radioactive to the fairer sex then. Next time we make up for it with the tragicomedic tale of how I finally did pop my cherry, and finally got my life on the road.

Fun Bum Presents ...tion Book

— HEY MOTHERFUCKER! WHaT are You LooKing at ?

The Trial of LicKey Louse

by Vava

NYSID
MANUFACTURED BY
PRODUCTION UNLIMITED
JEFFERSON REHABILITATION CENTER
WATERTOWN, NY 13601

THEY PUT HIM IN THE "Dark prison" right next to the BQE for some kind of "crime against the state." You think it's coincidence that he's a lapsed Muslim?

NEXT: "WHALE POLITICS"

Congratulations!
You're part of the problem!

Were you among that group of city dwellers who avoided the park at Wall Street in 2011 because of your abhorrence of homeless individuals?

Are you the sort who turns up your nose at crusty punks?

Did you think that that was the only sort of person who was down at Liberty Plaza? And if it had been, would you consider questioning your preconceptions about the worth of human individuals? No? Oy, for Pete's sake!

Well, now look what you bought yourself! You might have redeemed your politics five years ago, but instead, by ignoring what was going on, you have a demagogue for a president and a nation of disenfranchised and angry people. Couldn't we have done something to stop this then?

Buy this book and try to get a grip on yourself!

不合作方式[1]

or

WE
TAKE
UP
TROWELS

An action review by
Anicula

THE WORLD sees fire best, and always pricks up its ears to the shattering of glass. It is muffled cries that will not do, for the state, and the status quo, will always ignore what it can.

That sound is captured in the three still frames of the piece in question, *Dropping a Han Dynasty Urn*. The artist, Ai Weiwei, stands stock still in the center of the picture plane with a priceless ancient urn in his hands, and stares into our eyes with his own eyes somber, unfriendly, tired and pouched, and his lips set stern and unyielding. Down the urn drops. Ai's hands outward on either side, in suspension with the urn, which will fall. And then smashed at his feet; Ai stands unchanged, the urn not so. The artist must have blood of ice, we think, and this is a confrontation that clearly we, those watching, have lost.

The urn was dropped in 1995, at which point Ai had already witnessed his father, the poet Ai Qing, pass a lifetime in confrontation with the state. Ai Qing, a Communist loyalist, was in the government's good graces until his poetry ran afoul of some oblique boundary of taste and piety. In consequence, father and family both suffered exile and torment, and the world seemed to rise against Ai Qing—stones were thrown and black ink poured down his face (the tools of art weaponized; they did it first).[2] Many years more of this are in the offing for Ai Weiwei, who can't know his future, but looks from this picture as though he might. The man before us is mature and has no illusions, neither of hope nor of vanity, gone gently to seed with his stout frame and slipping face. Not a provocation by a young buck—enfant terrible, art world cliché—not teenage disillusionment, nihilism, but the statement of a man about his situation, a statement of cold-blooded lucidity. Without play-acting, he simply drops the vase. He is well aware of what he does.

An artist cannot help but understand the import of dropping such a thing. "The ritualized destruction of such objects could only be sanctioned by someone with a capacity like an emperor's to recognize and possess such prized

[1] Bù hé zuò fāng shì. Translation: "Methods of Non-Cooperation," the title of a 2000 exhibit curated by Ai Weiwei. English title: "Fuck Off."

[2] Evan Osnos, "It's Not Beautiful: An Artist Takes on the System," *New Yorker*, May 24, 2010. "When the Cultural Revolution began, things worsened. Ai Qing's tormentors poured ink on his face, and children threw stones at him. He and his family were sent to an area known as little Siberia, on the edge of the Gobi Desert, where they had to live in an underground cavern that had been used as a birthing place for farm animals. They were there for five years."

For a long period in his career, desecration was Ai Weiwei's métier.

works."[3] An emperor spends his leisure time in a reverie of acquisition and admiration, contemplating the beauty of his collections, but the artist who makes such things spends his days in physical pursuit of immortality. In solipsistic repose, the artist worries over the destruction of the world, for what will happen to his works then?[4] Will they send them out to space in a ship, or will they be bumped from this final journey by people and creatures?[5] Art makes it to the present or the future always against defying odds, as it is the entropic destiny of matter to degrade. The controversy of Ai's act is most controversial to the artist, of all people. Who cares more than he?

Art as unholy destruction elicits a reaction in all but lunatics; that is the purpose of it, after all. The reaction is somewhere on the continuum with works that go fur-

ther: Tom Otterness's 1978 piece *Shot Dog Film*, for instance, that depicts the artist killing a dog, the brutality and meaninglessness of which has haunted Otterness and his career for the last forty years. The specter of it has overshadowed all he's done since, even as he's moved on to projects that concern themselves with the betterment of The People and the elevation of the lower classes.[6]

For a long period in his career, desecration was Ai's métier. His massive retrospective at the Brooklyn Museum in 2014, *According to What?*, displayed all manner of banged-up antiquity: vases dripped in house paint (*Colored Vases*, 2007–10) and a vase on which he had painted the Coca Cola symbol (*Coca Cola Vase*, 2007), a work that seemed a bit too trite in 2007 to warrant a defilement of that extremity.

Humanists, people who care

---

[3] Gregg Moore and Richard Torchia, "Doing Ceramics," in *Ai Weiwei: Dropping the Urn* (Glenside, PA: Arcadia University Art Gallery, 2010).

[4] See *Life After People*, a television show on the History Channel, for a disturbing sense of how long it would be before all printed copies of Shakespeare's works would disintegrate without human intervention.

[5] Arkady and Boris Strugatsky, *Far Rainbow*, Trans. by Gary Kern (New York: Macmillan, 1979). "In town the main street was decorated by the paintings that the artists were exhibiting for the last time—leaning up against tree trunks, buildings, on wires across the street, and on lamp posts. People stood in front of paintings, remembering, quietly rejoicing, and a man was arguing loudly, and a pretty[,] thin woman cried bitterly, 'What a shame . . . what a shame!'"

[6] See Otterness's 1992 installation *The Real World* in Battery Park for a glimpse of how much one's intent can change over a lifetime.

about "human interests, values and dignity over all else," according to our friends at the big black doorstop and toddler hoister that is Webster's Unabridged, cannot ally themselves with such things, not comfortably. Smashing or painting over the works of ancient human history seems to fly in the face of all three of these standards. It feels worse still, now in 2017, living as we do in times when this simple pledge, affiliating ourselves with this most humble of principles—the dignity of human life and the importance of values—has become again radical, revolutionary. From all corners, apostates to humanism come to destroy our most beautiful treasures: our children, our art, the values of freedom and liberty.

All around us these things now fall. Look to 2001 when the Taliban blasted from their mountain in Afghanistan the Bamiyan Buddhas, 174-foot statues which had survived through 1500 years unharmed. ISIS, that modern enemy of sense and freedom, has looted and destroyed completely: Palymyra, Mar Elian Monastery, Apamae, Dura-Europos, Mari, Hatra, Ninevah, the Mosul Museum and Libraries, Nimrud, Khorsabad, Mar Behnam Monastery, the Mosque of the Prophet Yunus, Imam Dur Mausoleum.[7] Cities famous from the Bible, artifacts and buildings, old books, manuscripts, statues. Our own despoliation of the environment, no less criminal, has led to 93% of the Great Barrier Reef bleached and dying,[8] to the endangerment of giraffes, bees, and on and on. All across the spectrum of humanity, we live for destruction.

But Ai's piece is from a very different time period, and actions from twenty years ago had a different valence in their moment than they do when we look at them today. 1995 gazed backward, and a preoccupation with the past was evident in Ai's work as well. Most critics who remark on *Dropping the Urn* say it evokes the horrors of the Cultural Revolution in China, a time in which cultural artifacts, culture in general, and those who trafficked in it all were dropped from great heights. It is a disturbing prospect that Ai would do just exactly what he deplored, taking part in a destruction of cultural artifacts, on the face of it not so different from that

---

[7]Andrew Curry, "Here Are the Ancient Sites ISIS Has Destroyed," *National Geographic*, September 1, 2015.

[8]Brian Kahn, "Bleaching Hits 93 Percent of the Great Barrier Reef: Aerial Surveys Reveal that the Giant Coral Reef is Suffering Under Global Warming," *Scientific American*, April 20, 2016.

of the Communists. As Dario Gamboni puts it in his essay on Ai's iconoclasm, "Such a work raises an intriguing and possibly disturbing question:

Many people can kill a human being, it seems, but it takes a special madman to kill a work of art.

protect and care for the important products of our culture—our culture's soul—in times of fascism and nihilistic destruction. And we would imagine, as well, that those how could someone whose father and whose own youth suffered so much from the Maoist campaign for 'breaking down the Four Olds' (including the 'old culture') do something that would appear to some as a 'reenactment'—though admittedly on a small scale—of the same inept destruction?"[9] Gamboni notes: "The Four Olds were old ideas, old habits, old customs, and old culture. David Spalding wrote that Ai 'remarked on the loss of China's cultural legacy by reenacting its destruction.'"

The reification of these particular traumatic events, trauma done to culture, could seem to have little cultural value itself. One might suppose that it is the job of the humanist (a title that naturally attaches itself to artists) to

who have lived through such experiences see the necessity even more clearly. One thinks of the YIVO supporters in Nazi Germany who saved books and papers from the *Einsatzstab Reichsleiter Rosenberg* (ERR) whose task was to collect art and such from around Europe but who intended to shred all of YIVO's paper works,[10] or the many people throughout Europe, soldiers and civilians alike, who saved and protected paintings and other artwork, evacuating, sandbagging, lugging it around, and hunting it down when the war was over. There are people who would die to maintain the integrity and safety of art, just as there are those who perhaps more understandably would give their lives to protect other people. Why continue

---

[9]Dario Gamboni, "Ai Weiwei: Portrait of the Artist as an Iconoclast," in *Ai Weiwei: Dropping the Urn*.

[10]"YIVO during WWII," YIVO Institute, 2017, http://yivo.org. "The Jews assigned by the Nazis to sort through the archival and library materials risked their lives to hide rare artifacts. Calling themselves 'the Paper Brigade,' they smuggled books and papers to hiding places in the Jewish ghetto and the homes of friendly non-Jews. They concealed documents under floorboards and in walls and buried them in secret underground bunkers."

"Some members of the Paper Brigade were also members of the Vilna ghetto's Jewish resistance organization. They saw the rescue of Jewish cultural treasures as no less a holy mission than that of mounting an armed uprising against the Nazis."

to do that which has horrified us the most, that which seems to call our basic humanity into question? Many people can kill a human being, it seems, but it takes a special madman to kill a work of art.[11]

Although an only minimally accomplished sophist can do so easily—what after all can't theory of one kind or another be used to defend?—on some level *Dropping the Urn* is hard to support. The destruction of art and artifacts has a certain resonance that breaks through the torpor and shroud surrounding even real human deaths. Adults are used to hearing about wars and murder. If we never became inured to some measure of it, we would have a hard time going on.

On some level we know that we all must come and go, but the remnants of our existences give us some kind of hope. We die but we contribute to the future in some way, or at least our civilizations do. We leave behind aqueducts and vases and bas-reliefs, even if it is inevitable that our bones break down and the dust takes us, leaving not even the shadows of Nagasaki or the negative spaces of limbs and open mouths that the people of Pompeii left behind.

Before Ai focused on the destruction and desecration of ancient Chinese pottery, his project was the counterfeiting of such pottery, using artisans from around China to make work according to the ancient standards. As Philip Tinari points out, his constructions served a similarly destructive purpose, though one more theoretical and less literal: "[the care with which the reproductions are pursued flies in the face of] the prolonged emphasis on the 'fake,' which pronounced in the Mandarin pinyin syllables that spell it is a homophone for that other great modality in Ai's work, 'fuck.' As originally posited, 'fake' and 'fuck' are one in [sic] the same: to counterfeit objects of great purported economic and cultural value was to fly in the face of hierarchies of price and approbation. In this logic, fakeness is an absolute condition in opposition to the genuine, and to embrace it is a move as much gestural as substantive, a way of declaring one's independence (in the western liberal tradition) or 'unwillingness to cooperate' (in the Chinese *jianghu* tradition)."[12]

---

[11] Moore and Torchia, "Doing Ceramics." "Smashing ancient ceramics is not something that anyone can do. 'People just can't release their hands and let gravity do the work,' continued Ai, defending the license to destroy that expertise grants him. 'I never hesitated.'"

[12] Philip Tinari, "Postures in Clay: The Vessels of Ai Weiwei," Arcadia University, 2010, http://www.arcadia.edu.

There is a point, Ai seems to say, when pointed destruction is the only sane response.

The "hierarchies of price and approbation" are demolished by creating and honoring (with the care it took to build them accurately) facsimiles and their production. By honoring the process of creating facsimiles, and by presenting them as art works in their own right, we flip off the system. Honoring and caring for a value so at odds with our own system of valuation is a way to declare ourselves free of and separate from the system and all that goes along with it, i.e., "If you honor that, I'll honor the opposite."

As Gamboni phrases it, the question of perception and value-making in Ai's work is laid entirely on the back of the viewer: "The question 'what am I doing?' that the artist pictured in *Dropping a Han-Dynasty Urn* seems to be asking from us can thus be rephrased: 'What do you want me to be doing?'" But another question poses itself which is: If this (i.e., the facsimiles, the urn) is not of value (which it is clearly not, in the case of the dropped urn, since Ai is destroying it), then what is? The question may have a nihilistic answer—though I doubt it. Ai's constant flipping of the bird (literally in his *Study of Perspective* series (1995–2003), metaphor-ically elsewhere in his work) wears on one, in much the same way as the words of a teenage suburban juvenile delinquent shouting at old people outside of a 7/11, but I don't think the answer for him lies there. Ai's later body of work expresses a different set of values entirely: productive and forceful, presenting belief in something.

Ai's attention and activism, and accordingly his work, gained an urgency and focus in 2008 when an earthquake in Sichuan, China killed around 90,000 people, over 5,000 of whom were children. Ai, who had already been using the internet as a platform, angered authorities by collecting the names of the children who had died and posting them to his blog. The children had attended poorly built schools, and the government wished to paper over its clear responsibility for their deaths. Ai spent years of his life remembering and honoring the students in video projects, installations of twisted metal from the site, and audio recordings. At his retrospective *According to What?*, Ai installed a piece in memory of the children, *Snake Ceiling*. It began with 360 identical children's backpacks that Ai found at the site of the earthquake. All of this came at a great personal cost to him, too, as these works and his research into the identity of the children triggered an extreme response from the government. He was beaten by the police so badly that the beating triggered a brain aneurysm that required later surgery, and he was imprisoned—disappeared, in effect—for over 80 days.[13]

So what does Ai value? Human life, human dignity, freedom, and noncompliance even with art itself. Ai's credo over the course of a varied art career and consistent mounting activism seems to fall not far from one voiced by that holy fool Sid Vicious: "Undermine their pompous authority, reject their moral standards, make anarchy and disorder your trademarks. Cause as much chaos and disruption as possible but don't let them take you alive." When their careless use of authority leads to death and their self-protection suffocates freedom of speech, when their false moral dictates stand in opposition to true morality, then anarchy and disorder can feel like the only response. This is true in the works Ai has made, as well as in his behavior. At times he has taken the op-posite tack by trying to work with the government, only to end up repudiating his own actions.[14]

Though later he would react differently to the provocations of the government, *Dropping a Han-Dynasty Urn* is that sort of response. Smash the state, the old anarchist credo goes. "When they kick out your front door, how you gonna come? With your hands on your head, or on the trigger of your gun?" There is a moment, Ai seems to say with the photos, when pointed destruction is the only sane response. And more importantly, it is the only response that will elicit a reaction. The dropping of the urn is the point at the party when the glass breaks: The room goes quiet and, despite themselves, everybody turns to look. You turn instinctively to look. The fact that the piece was undertaken spontaneously "to test a new camera," as Ai claims, does not change the intentionality. The anger and defiance were already there, or he never would have dropped it. Later he built things, but first he kicked the windows out.

The association of Ai with punk ideology is certainly fair. Fair

---

[13] Melissa Block, "In 'According to What?' Ai Weiwei Makes Mourning Subversive," *All Things Considered*, podcast audio, January 23, 2013, http://www.npr.org.

[14] "China Artist Ai Weiwei says he regrets designing Beijing Olympics Bird's Nest," *Telegraph*, March 5, 2012, http://www.telegraph.co.uk.

[15] James Panero, "The New Political Art: On Ai Weiwei, Pussy Riot and the Right Way to do Political Art," *New Criterion*, September 2012.

enough that this is not the first time it's been suggested.[15] Ai lived in New York City from 1981 to 1993, and as an artist kicking around downtown, he was present for a New York City punk scene as well as the later days of some early radicals like Allen Ginsberg. He marked his presence with photos of the Tompkins Square Park riots, art about AIDS,[16] and generally did what artists did back then in New York City, made art and involved himself in the underground of the city. He was also, and continues to be, an outspoken critic of Communist China and its attitudes toward its artists and citizens, its violent ways of silencing dissidents, its imperviousness. He has been jailed and hounded for his work and outspokenness, but has continued to do his work, and has become no less outspoken.

Let's define our terms, though: What is it to be a punk? "If you want to understand the potent values of punk, confront taboos, do not tolerate hypocrisy, investigate the truth for yourself." So says Joe

"Punk was never, never meant to be nostalgic."

Corre, whose bona fides include being the progeny of punk fashion designer Vivienne Westwood and punk fashion and music impresario (and sometime conman, humbug, and disco opera composer[17]) Malcolm McLaren. Corre has made millions moving high-end undergarments for his company Agent Provocateur, and at the same time has balanced his karma by speaking out on fracking and capitalistic excess, rejecting the MBE in 2007 in protest over Britain's involvement in Iraq.

This past fall, Corre was pricked to action and defiance again by an unfortunate fortieth anniversary being marked in London. It seems that the Sex Pistol's *Anarchy in the UK* is 40 years old, and all of London is very excited about it. Or at least a very particular set of the cultural elite, who have seen no irony at all in their round of establishment events commemorating this anniversary. The exhibit comes at a time, Corre tells us, when "you can buy McDonald's Punky Nuggets[18] and *Anar-*

---

[16]See his piece *Safe Sex* from 1986. It is a raincoat with a condom attached at about crotch level.

[17]See Malcolm McLaren's album *Fans* (Island Records, 1984).

[18]True or not, or merely poetic license, I can find no reference to them.

[19]This is, most remarkably, true. Put out by Virgin, who describe them thusly: "They challenged convention and the established way of thinking—just as we are doing today in our quest to shake up UK banking." Pure self-parody, maybe, but in existence nevertheless.

[20]Iggy Pop has begun shilling for Swiftcover car insurance. The advertisement is un-

chy in the UK credit cards at 19% APR,[19] punk-rock car insurance,[20] and bondage trousers from Louis Vuitton."[21]

Corre would have us know, however, that "Punk was never, never meant to be nostalgic. And you can't learn to be one at a Museum of London workshop." Be that as it may, that is just what the good people of London would like to do about it, for the Museum of London is offering any number of nice, state-sanctioned workshops on the topic this year.

Corre, as the child of two such personages, entwined as they both were in the origins of London punk, is in possession of a tremendous collection of punk memorabilia, so tremendous that it is worth an estimated five million pounds,[22] and to the shock and horror of some in the community of people watching him, he set fire to this collection of punk paraphernalia on a barge in the middle of the Thames on November 7th (a date that is, of course, quite close to one that will live in infamy for the American people. But that is for a later discussion). On YouTube, you can also watch him

burning a "one-of-a-kind acetate of *Anarchy in the UK*" for a preliminary of what was soon to come.

As might be imagined, people were pissed. If negative comments under a video on YouTube are any indication of public opinion at large, the negative comments under the video of the action went as follows:

Flaskamel: "Tomorrow nobody will care about this. What a waste of time."

Andres Barriga: "I love the punk attitude. But wouln't [sic] it have been better to sell it all and use the money on a good cause? This is a powerful statememt [sic], but achieves almost nothing."

Padraic O'Donoghue: "And you achieved what by doing this? You fucking piece of shit. Punk means alot [sic] to me and millions like me this means fuck all just some jumped up spoiled brat looking for attention."

tracksofnyc: "I see a lot of nothing. What a waste."

Pedro Perrito: "spoilt brat..."

Too, the action was largely ignored by anyone but the press. Though it was widely publicized beforehand, besides journalists, no

---

believable and I suggest you check it out on YouTube. I suppose it could be considered on-brand for him, as he is originally from Detroit.

[21] Burn Punk London, "BURN PUNK OCTOPUS TV live stream 26th November 2016," YouTube video, November 26, 2016, http://www.youtube.com.

[22] Christopher D. Shea, "To Save Punk's Soul, a Bonfire of Some of Its Vanities on the Thames," *New York Times*, November 7, 2016.

masses showed up either to support his actions or to boo him vociferously. It seemed most particularly that those who were so excited to see punk deified in the British Museum could not genuinely perceive a punk act when it was right before them.

Can punk be present in memorabilia or is it impossible to contain?

The Punk London website itself, clearly chafed, linked to an extreme hatchet job by a writer for Noisey called "An Ass on the River: Pulling Back the Curtain on the £5-Million Punk Burning."[23] The author, Oscar Rickett, calls Corre out for his extreme privilege and money, and calls out those watching, associates of Corre's, for things like their £6-thousand bear fur coats. He also derides Corre for his rambling, a vice that, it must be noted, in no way excludes him from being the mouthpiece of any opposition movement.

This all, the gossiping opinion of the commentariat, only obliquely touches on the validity and strength of the action itself. Was the action worthwhile? Did it garner attention and awareness for its subject? Corre's privilege does in no way undo his ability to see the reality of our collective problem. As Dullcharlie says in the comments beneath the video: "And what does [punk] mean to you? The music? The message? The spirit? Or some old clothes, bits of paper and records that you were never going to own, see or hear anyway?" Can punk be present in memorabilia and artifacts or is it, as Corre's action states plainly, impossible to contain in things like that?

Since we are in fact taking time to review the action, the effectiveness of the protest has to be analyzed under two rubrics: Was this punk? And was this effective as an action? Fede018 opines: "Corre pissing people off by setting shit on fire IS punk!" and I tend to agree with him. £6-thousand bear fur coats or no, this protest is punk as fuck.

There are effigies of British politicians. There are four grim reapers holding signs printed on red flags. There is an enormous banner that says: "Extinction! Your future." There is another enormous sign that is a map of the world. At the top is the legend, "Red = uninhabitable land at +5 degrees." On bottom: "We can't stop it once it reaches +2 degrees."

---

[23] Oscar Rickett, "An Ass on the River: Pulling Back the Curtain on the £5-Million Punk Burning," *Noisey*, November 29, 2016, http://noisey.vice.com.

There is a guy playing a drum kit. There are flames and firecrackers that go off when the effigies are ignited. And, of course, there is the fact that it is on the barge in the middle of the Thames, which is, at the very least, delightful.

For my money, Corre has a cogent argument, well argued: "London is being socially cleansed and turned into a theme park." True in New York, true in Paris, true in London. Corre goes on to say, "Some people are very concerned about the price of these artifacts, but the conversation we need to have is about values." In the spirit of constructive politics, Corre even offers up a solution: "So what can we do? Stop buying their lies. And stop buying their products." Street theater and a good show underscore bigger issues and challenge wider beliefs and expectations. The Left, in the form of one angry brassiere peddler, goes on the offensive.

In cultures of restraint, either state-mandated, as in the case of Ai, or those created with extreme social pressure, as in our western internet-driven late capitalism, these acts ring loudly. A punk within the context of a wider mass movement acts under cover of a mob, thereby compromising, on some level, his ability to act outside of and against the status quo. He is a member of *a* status quo,

if not *the* status quo. The person who walks alone to the center of the public eye to deliver their own message without the support of the like-minded sets himself up for all manner of vilification, without any cover at all from either the state, in the case of Ai, or from the disapprobrium of the people, as in the case of Corre. (which is punk as fuck)

❧

CODA: The more I consider the problem of smashing things up, the more I'm disturbed by my findings. A changed landscape requires a change in tactics, and one can't plot one's course with an outdated map any more than one can build up a successful opposition with an old notion of one's enemy.

The problem we face now is unspeakably more urgent than it was on November 7th, when Corre took to his barge to burn his ephemera. Not only are the stakes much higher, but we are forced to exhaust the bulk of our energy in defensive action, spending our strength on battles for things and ideas that feel like they should be matters of common ground for all adults, no matter their side of the political spectrum (libraries, science itself, a woman's right not to be grabbed at. Basic aspects of a civilized modern society.) Resistance has become more complicated, tedious and pressing than it was at the end of 2016, or perhaps and more likely, it is only more apparent to us now what it actually entails. The current president was elected, after all, because the ground was somehow laid for him.

When did the Right become iconoclasts and the Left the party of conservatives? This is an alteration of landscape that began, this time around in the cycle of history, with the Tea Party, and has led now to a seismic shift. We are in a peculiar situation, and one for which we are characterologically ill-suited. Modern activists are most comfortable working towards the end of the status quo. "Outgrow the Status Quo," says an Occupy poster in my own dining room. We have never, or at least not in my memory, been faced with the question of how or what to build. We are not used to feeling a tender love toward the values of our country, toward those slave-holding founding fathers our side has long repudiated.[24] Toward the court system!

I walked past the home of one of the federal judges who helped strike down the first travel ban recently, and seeing the cop car positioned outside for more than a week, and knowing the danger she might be in, I felt a soaring of patriotism in my chest. I'm put in mind of a story told by Mark Twain. Far from home on a ship in the Strait of Gibraltar, he came upon another American ship, an encounter full of pleasure and real warmth.[25] But the foreign waters are our own country, and the passing American ships people of right mind, former strangers, who have just begun to recognize each other!

Out on a main thoroughfare in Brooklyn recently, a young man and woman in corporate-activist t-shirts were raising money for the fight against the Trump administration. A belligerent man with a carry-out tray of Starbucks cof-

---

[24] For this we have Lin-Manuel Miranda to thank. "Hercules Mulligan, I need no introduction. When you knock me down I get the fuck back up again."

[25] Mark Twain, *Innocents Abroad* (New York: Penguin, 2002). "But while we stood admiring the cloud-capped peaks and the lowlands robed in misty gloom a finer picture burst upon us and chained every eye like a magnet—a stately ship, with canvas piled on canvas till she was one towering mass of bellying sail! She came speeding over the sea like a great bird. Africa and Spain were forgotten. All homage was for the beautiful stranger. While everybody gazed she swept superbly by and flung the Stars and Stripes to the breeze! Quicker than thought, hats and handkerchiefs flashed in the air, and a cheer went up! She was beautiful before—she was radiant now. Many a one on our decks knew then for the first time how tame a sight his country's flag is at home compared to what it is in a foreign land. To see it is to see a vision of home itself and all its idols, and feel a thrill that would stir a very river of sluggish blood!"

Our adversaries have stolen chaos from us, and we cannot ask for it back.

fees, for his office, one supposes, shouted at them as he passed by: "I support the Trump administration! You should support your country!"

It is evident to everyone who has been out in the street or obsessively refreshing their computers to sign new petitions or calling their representatives on speed dial that they are supporting their country. They have considered America's values, and are laboring to maintain them. It is the other side that clearly wants to pull them down. They have said as much. The state itself—or at least that cabal with which Mr. Trump surrounds himself—now seems to have made anarchy its business. The Right has taken over the Left's modus operandi. Their job as they see it is to take the whole thing apart. As Steve Bannon, Trump's primary appointed lunatic, said recently at the 2017 CPAC conference: "The third, broadly, line of work is deconstruction of the administrative state. . . . If you look at these cabinet appointees, they were selected for a reason and that is the de-construction. The way the progressive left runs, is if they can't get it passed, they're just going to put in some sort of regulation in an agency. That's all going to be deconstructed. . . ."[26]

When questioned as to why he hadn't staffed so many positions in his administration—as of the hundred-day mark there are still hundreds of positions unstaffed—the president stated: "In many cases, we don't want to fill those jobs. A lot of those jobs I don't want to appoint because they're unnecessary to have."[27] It is a small step between the traditional Republican desire for small government and this newer idea, a skeleton crew headed up by a bantam-weight strongman, our own, most un-American, autocrat pretendu. Even pirate ships, history tells us, employed some sort of democratic proceedings.[28]

It now falls on us to be builders and defenders against ruffians and anarchists. Whether we like it or not, we must be the ones to love and care for our institutions. They—Trump, Bannon, the lot of

---

[26] Max Fisher, "Stephen K. Bannon's CPAC Comments, Annotated and Explained," *New York Times*, February 24, 2017.

[27] Josh Barro, "Trump Is Taking His Time to Fill More Than 500 Key Jobs, and That Could Stymie His Agenda," *Business Insider*, February 28, 2017.

[28] "Study: Pirates Pursued Democracy, Helped American Colonies Survive," University of Florida, June 28, 2006, http://news.ufl.edu.

them—are the Black Bloc anarchists with their faces covered by bandanas. We leftists are the homeowners and bourgeoisie who wish to have lawns and salubrious milk for children, lending libraries, parks to walk our dogs, cool evening temperatures, frozen ice caps. In other words, order, not chaos. Ghosts of Stonewall brick throwers, football-helmeted Weathermen, Sacco and Vanzetti's kinsmen with homespun incendiaries must haunt another world beyond the veil. Our adversaries have stolen chaos from us, and we cannot ask for it back.

So what is left to us well-intentioned adults who do not want to burn down the branches of government and our country's freedoms along with them? They have taken destruction, anger and militancy, and left us holding the American flag. We mill around with our pins and our ACLU-printed copies of the constitution ($11.99 for 10, a good price) in our back pockets like the hankies that gay men used to display while cruising. "The left-hand side signifies that I believe Dissent is Patriotic."

It is left to us to do the quiet work that does not draw the eye: Raise funds, architect new institutions that can't easily be displaced, make plans for the future, build infrastructure and alliances between movements, publish, educate, and hold fast to America and the values we cherish. That is to say, to do the work of upstanders, work that is mostly without flash, glamor or frisson. Community boards, unions, local politics. Reinvest these humble parts of a functioning democracy with energy and force. Wear out our shoe leather in institutional halls.

It seems we no longer have the luxury to smash anything at all. The nihilistic pain-sowers of the world, from ISIS to Breitbart, are now in league, and they have that side of things on lock. ℰ

Ballpoint Perps!

Oct. 30
Rogelio
Age 71
Participation
in Staged Motor
Vehica Cras
P.O.B. CC

IT TAKES 5 SECONDS

T HESE "Sharp Cards" should be used for your own revolutionary purposes: collect and trade them, xerox and hand them out to friends and neighbors, or stick one in your child's lunch box along with her defrosted edamame! As the collection grows over the months, you will even have enough cards to flip!

Gene Sharp, the namesake of this collection, founded the Albert Einstein Institute, so named because Einstein, an advocate for peace, wrote the introduction to Sharp's first book, on Gandhi. Sharp's life's work is writing, researching and disseminating the history and methods of nonviolent re- sistance in such books and pamphlets as *From Dictatorship to Democracy* and *The Politics of Nonviolent Action*, from which the methods depicted on the cards have been drawn. Sharp has been rightly nominated four times for the Nobel Peace Prize.

Before handing them out, we like to paint the cards with watercolors. We recommend purple as the color for the resistance fist, a color favored by Food Not Bombs, among others, and one which represents all of us, or none of us in particular.

We hope these cards will both amuse and hearten you, but most of all we hope to see you in the streets! ℯ

COURAGE!

Your hands may tremble but they have strength in them!

In the darkest times in human history people have found ways to fight back and win, over unwinnable odds, against enemies that were just as insidious, malevolent, and powerful as your own, and sometimes moreso!

All around you are friends and allies, people who wish you well, who care about you, and who have common cause with you.

The arc of history bends towards justice, but it is because people bend it themselves.

Dry your eyes and hurry!

Issued by:

MATCHLOCK PRESS

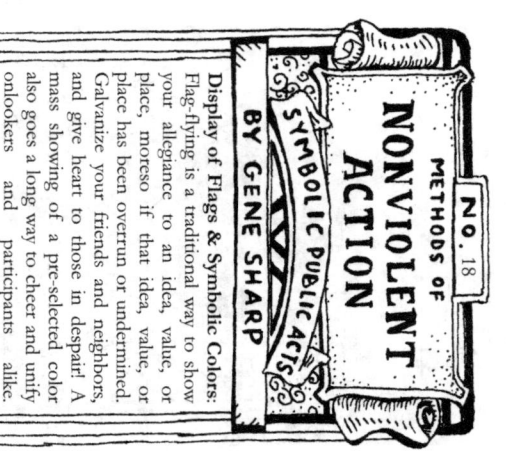

NO. 18

METHODS OF

NONVIOLENT ACTION

SYMBOLIC PUBLIC ACTS

BY GENE SHARP

Display of Flags & Symbolic Colors: Flag-flying is a traditional way to show your allegiance to an idea, value, or place, moreso if that idea, value, or place has been overrun or undermined. Galvanize your friends and neighbors, and give heart to those in despair! A mass showing of a pre-selected color also goes a long way to cheer and unify onlookers and participants alike.

ISSUED BY

MATCHLOCK PRESS

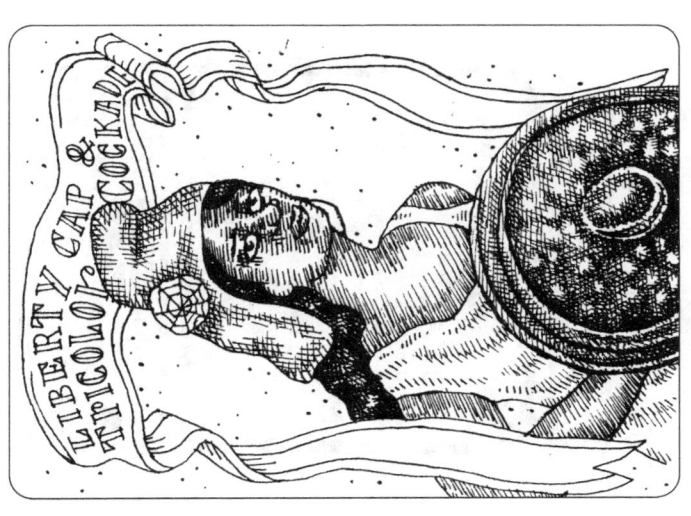

LIBERTY CAP & TRICOLOr COCKADE

Community group Leaders
Advancing & Helping Communities,
rejects $500,000 in federal aid.

Suehaila Amen, board member
DEARBORN, MI 2017

○Wearing of Symbols: When you grow weary of shouting, a symbol can speak for you. Symbols worn on the body have helped people across many resistance movements to announce their own positions and reach out to each other. Flowers in buttonholes, hats of all kinds, and even paper clips stuck in lapels have all served this duty. When you wear a symbol, allys will turn up all around you. Who knows but that a nod of the head or bright knowing smile from a stranger might be heartening enough to keep you in the fight another day?

Adapted from

GENE SHARP

ISSUED BY : Matchlock Press

THE METHODS OF
NONVIOLENT ACTION

53.

Withdrawal & Renunciation:

Renouncing Honors:
It is unnatural for human beings to rebuff honors and tokens of respect, especially if they are hard won, which is what makes the renunciation of honors such a powerful and thought-provoking act. Things that once meant a lot can cease to have any meaning at all when the information about them changes. Some people of conscience choose to turn their backs on ego and hypocrisy in this eloquent way.

ISSUED BY
MATCHLOCK PRESS

Meet the BEST ping pong player on Sobek!

Read all about Fmr. Ambassador Qui-deeé in the pages of
"Homesick for Earth" by Olivia Schanzer

To Land a Man

A novel by
Olivia Schanzer

II

NEW YORK, the city where Mrs Wallace lived, was a much changed thing since her earlier days. She need not walk very far out of her door to be reminded of it. She was on her way to her club to attend a board meeting, but to get where she was due, she was forced to go at least six blocks out of her way, for there were certain places she refused to pass.

It was true that the modern era would not allow its invitation declined; it was the most infuriating and tenacious of suitors. It did not matter that one had made one's intentions clear, for the Aughts were quite deaf to one's own desires, and whistled loudly over one's protestations; it felt sure it had claimed one and that was enough. Clearly, the time she lived in—just past the millennium and not a thing to show for it—would not rest until the worst of its trappings was as familiar as one's own face; more so, as one had to go out of one's way to catch sight of oneself in a mirror.

Like that suitor, it had to know that it was despised, yet here it foisted its advertisements and the lettering of its signs upon one, as if it could not help but woo, most especially, those unwilling. Mrs Wallace, like the girl burdened socially with this sort of affection, who cannot make the boy relent, try as she might, and must therefore do her best to avoid the places he frequents, found herself avoiding those city blocks on which she would find what she so hated, which was any of the modern industries.

Yet here were society's cheap hamburgers, swaddled in garish plastic, and its portable telephones and firm order of storefronts, replicated in infinite regression, as if every block were Louis XIV looking into his own foul vanity in the Hall of Mirrors. Perhaps one might become tricked into camaraderie because one was familiar. Mrs Wallace, who found this same enemy lurking in her pantry whenever she was not explicit with her shopping list (for the woman who did the shopping did not see how a simple box of crackers might be a profound intrusion, when packaged in the modern style) did not mistake the two; she could not be made to call contempt tolerance. The English language had not been bungled as badly as that.

It was a saving grace that there would always be side streets on which to linger, and Mrs Wallace reassured herself that it was not possible for the commercial shadow to cast a pall over every inch of the city. They could not raze brownstones to make room for shops, after all; they could not be that greedy for these replicated shops. Surely her neighbors would not allow them to put up advertisements along their cornices, either; even the worst of them was not that crass.

On streets all around the club where Mrs Wallace went now for her meeting, the old places had been shuttered and replaced, and the men and women who had run them, many with whom she had been quite familiar, had gone on, to where she did not know. The man who had called himself Monsieur Parapluie—for his little shop sold only umbrellas—who liked to shake the children's hands quite formally when they visited with their mothers, came first to mind when she thought of them. Yet the club did not attend at all to these worldly eradications.

The club had stood for one hundred years in stone dignity upon this same foundation, and it was defiant of the block on which it stood. It took only the barest notice of the skyscraper going up on the corner, which was to say occasionally it covered the windows facing that site

to prevent the dust from getting in, but this it did as discreetly as a person putting a handkerchief to his mouth when he coughed. It did not waste, beyond that, any opinion on the subject.

The only change that had occurred in this well-proportioned building in all the years it had stood at this spot had been to its name, for the club's only indecision was in knowing who precisely it was, not in being that thing. Over the years, it had been named both the Arts Club and the Crafts Club, as it changed its name according to whether the day's mania was literature or glass etching, and whether the membership held pretensions up or down. As both interests were now equally devalued by the times—Mrs Wallace noted that attending museums and painting on nuts were viewed as much the same thing by that younger generation— it was called the Arts and Crafts Club, and seemed to have settled with that.

The club maintained itself—even its flaws—in pleasing stasis. It seemed, save a bloody schism that Mrs Wallace could not foresee, that no great change could come within these walls. Therefore, if there were a member who cut into cake before it was due to be served, thirty years hence he would be cutting into cake that same way if the senility that prompted his behavior was slow to overtake him; he would not be drummed out for as little as this. This went as well for bylaws, no matter how ill-conceived (Was it really sense that some votes were taken twice, and some things decided by fiat? Or that junior members of the board were forced to leave that room when certain topics were discussed?), for rules, no matter how outmoded (Should visiting children only be allowed to order cheese sandwiches? Must the matron come along and tap them on the shoulder if they do not finish their milk, even if their mothers are seated there?), or social mores no matter how inexplicable (Though men no longer wore mustaches and had no cause for it, still every year at the winter meeting, all members present were warned against the use of mustache wax, for the behest of a deceased gentleman required it.).

The building itself was just as consistent. Here, no part of the décor had ever changed, and Mrs Wallace knew for certain that whatever was unscrewed from the wall, be it decorative or functional, would be repaired and put back again. Even the light switches in the bathrooms were not light switches but old-fash-ioned buttons that took some force to operate, the kind with which Mrs Wallace had grown up.

There were lamps in the lobby of such an age that Mrs Wallace's grandfather had been photographed beside one, his cigarette filling the lampshade with smoke. The lobby, with its green carpets and couches, seemed to age at its own elephantine pace with only infrequent and minor repairs; it lumbered so slowly toward decrepitude that it would never make it to that destination.

Mrs Wallace herself had decorated her house once, and now only moved things around slightly so as not to wear down the rugs. Seasonally, she replaced the dried hydrangea that stood in tall Chinese vases on either side of the living room fireplace with pussy willow, but that was the extent of it, for she thought little of variety for its own sake.

On either side of the marble stairs in the lobby of the club, there was and always had been a large bouquet which, using the same holy science for all those years, the same elderly woman had long found it her job to arrange. One must keep plucking at them so that they space themselves naturally; that was how the book from France explained to do it. One needn't stop again to ask her about it, when once one had done so, for there would not be any change in her answer even if thirty years divided one's inquiries.

The same, too, was the case for the library on the second floor—which Mrs Wallace now passed as she made her way to the boardroom—where the men and women smoked cigarettes at their leisure, and without that modern shame so prevalent, and which Mrs Wallace so deplored. Cigars were certainly allowed here, if one's guest asked. Mrs Wallace always greeted the man who sat watch on the periphery as she passed by the lounge—since she had quit smoking, most sadly, she had no cause to sit in there.

The men and women had their own separate rooms for lunch, which was a condition from the club's beginnings when they had known enough to demand safe haven from each other, and though the two rooms became one at dinner, the pocket doors between them were never opened between eleven-thirty and two on weekdays. Mrs Wallace did prefer her lunchtime talks with Larinda to remain undisturbed.

After entering the club, and with one's back toward the window—for the street was a variable factor and clearly could not be controlled; buses were always traveling by, bearing on their sides those wicked injunctions from which Mrs Wallace could not help but turn—it might be any year in the last century. Still, for all of this, the place was not unmixed tranquility for Mrs Wallace.

Within these walls, Mrs Wallace had a human enemy. She was not, in the world, alone in this, of course. Many were the people with enemies; many were the places so haunted. Yet this was not that common type of enemy. As proof, one need only look at that person's ten-year war against the Landmarks Commission, a war to raze the Thomas Stammler House at Seventy-Second Street, one which she waged for no sounder reason than that a very eccentric architect from abroad would have liked to build there; though it was a high-water mark of the nineteenth century, she did not care to see that house remain. This was that woman's type, not readily ignored.

That enemy had once been very near to Mrs Wallace, once had been every night within touching distance of her sleep, and eaten porridge every morning stirred in the same pot, and been patted at by the same maternal hands, the right to them possessed equally by each child. Now this board meeting she attended was the only place to see that woman and take stock, for they were both still members at their mother's club.

Certainly, she might see her when she and Mrs Chester crossed paths in the halls of that place, but there was no satisfaction in such a limited encounter. The meetings alone could bring that satisfaction. It was to examine her from a position across the boardroom table, Mrs Chester pinned to her seat securely by circumstance, that Mrs Wallace came eagerly to these meetings, and it was well worth the payment it exacted that she too would be examined.

Four times a year Mrs Wallace and her adversary sat across the boardroom table, took in each other's selection of jewelry, which, having once been owned in common, was a semaphore hoisted over their ships, a silent form of conversation, though unlike that other means, entirely private. Their mouths did not open to speak, yet the pin upon her adversary's bosom, which once had been her own, shone forth with spears of light, as intelligible as any language might have been.

Mrs Wallace now entered the boardroom and took her usual seat next to Larinda by the open window. Larinda had a very small committee to head, with only one other woman as member, and complained constantly over that woman's lack of investment, yet Mrs Wallace was very glad Larinda had reason to be there, as she was always in accord with Mrs Wallace; when Larinda was through with her own presentation, her role was to attend Mrs Wallace silently in freighted moments and to be a second pair of eyes, to hand Mrs Wallace her pen, and even, when necessary, to note down on paper what was said for later reflection. Larinda had an unerring sense of the sort of things upon which one might later like to reflect. Larinda, Mrs Wallace knew, in this and many other ways, played beautifully the role of adjutant, when called upon to do so.

The meeting—for though all present would have preferred it, it could not be composed solely of idle conversation—was called to order. As the budget was discussed, Mrs Wallace spent some time dwelling upon the placement of Mrs Chester's hands upon the table. Unlike the rest of the company, who held books and newspapers in their laps, Mrs Chester's hands lay above board and in plain sight. With that position, she laid her claim of ownership over a wide swath of space around her, and did not budge from it. It was pure presumption to take up as much space as Mrs Chester did, building impassable bulwarks with a series of folders she had brought along, yet there was not a board member nearby who would remark, for they were all excessively timid and, it seemed, even fearful of that woman. They seemed to feel they were lucky if she did not also demand from them their very chairs.

Next came the committee presentations. Mrs Wallace, who could imagine no other way, always went first. She did not monopolize, nor did she grandstand, simply spoke her piece and was done, as befitted her office. She had headed the Arts and Crafts committee for a very long time, and she did not flatter herself to say it was the most important of the committees, the oldest of them, and the one which conferred the most dignity on its members.

Mrs Wallace was also flattered to note, and glad to have Larinda corroborate, that hers was one of the few times during the meeting when it seemed the members put down their books and papers and attended to the speaker, and this fact alone, she felt, proved all that she believed on the subject of leadership.

If Mrs Wallace spoke lean words and sat before long, Mrs Chester always tried even those interested with her prolixity. It was a seasonal fact that Mrs Chester would declaim—one could do nothing about that—and it was fact, too, that the members put down their newspapers for her as well, though Mrs Wallace believed that, like her land grab on the boardroom table, Mrs Chester's audacity simply frightened the other members into it. And this perhaps proved to Mrs Chester all that she believed about leadership.

It was now Mrs Chester's turn to present. Mrs Chester was responsible, each year—with the purported help of outside forces, and what Mrs Wallace knew to be an extremely cowed committee—for selecting the recipient of the Timloe Stipend. The club had been giving it out to painters since Mr Timloe died in the late sixties, and as Mr Timloe had been something of a world traveler as well as a gentleman painter, the award had long gone to such as he. The mission statement, as printed on the top of the Timloe Stipend stationery— Mrs Chester's committee was alone in having this thing, as she alone had taken advantage of an interregnum period between treasurers to requisition it—was the simply stated: "A steady eye, a steady hand, and feet ever on the move." As far as Mrs Wallace could ascertain, they had always been most diligent in adhering to these limited standards.

Along with the money awarded—not a meager sum—came what Mrs Wallace had long characterized as an extremely grotesque party. This thing, too, Mrs Chester prepared.

Traditionally, Timloe family members, as well as the full committee, attended this fall board meeting, and every year it was usual for several candidates to be presented, discussed, and voted on there. This meant that in the yearly cycle of board meetings, Mrs Chester's presence was most fully felt in the autumn.

Mrs Wallace could see that woman sipping from her water, and rising now, and so she brought her attention away from mere thoughts of her, and to the person in the flesh. Lit up by the window, Mrs Chester's hair was golden, as lustrous a color as that element provided; it seemed as if that substance had been poured and fitted in defense of Mrs Chester's ears, which, oft-threatened, required some protection against blows aimed there.

"The Timloe Award cannot just go to any man, as it has in the past," began Mrs Chester, who had risen.

Across from Mrs Chester at the table there sat a very elderly woman, the late Mr Timloe's wife, who had come to hear how the late Mr Timloe's memory would be honored this year, and it was to her that Mrs Chester turned.

"Over the years, I have been very ashamed of some of our choices." Mrs Chester now leaned on the table, giving to Mrs Wallace the distinct impression of a shelf of rock hanging over some smaller thing, its connection to the greater mountain a moment from being severed. Mrs Wallace was not surprised to see Mrs Chester address herself in this way to the most vulnerable person in the room. The widow Timloe could not be very far from her centennial year.

"Our committee has never been accountable to a rigorous process of selection. It seemed in the past that we were expected by the older members of Mr Timloe's family to select the candidate they felt was best for the job," Mrs Chester continued on, rattling her saber. Mrs Wallace wondered if that thing might ever rust out and cease to sound.

"This year, however, our rigor has

been trebled. Although, of course, if there were no rigor initially, one could not say that we have trebled it. Let us say, instead, that we have trebled our own expectations for what this artist should be, which always were quite high, though perennially thwarted.

"The man we select this year will not be subject to your approval, Mrs Timloe, or to Mr Timloe's brother's approval. Your son, Mrs Timloe, a man with whom I bear a like mind, has agreed to our candidate already. He declared to me in no uncertain terms that he has long awaited this opportunity, and now speaks for all of you. You may take it up with him if that is not the case. I shall not inject myself between kin, or take up as my own that which is clearly an internal problem."

Mrs Timloe now gripped her pocketbook with two thin hands, and said, "I most certainly shall take it up with him."

"A letter has already been sent out to our honoree," said Mrs Chester, her eyes only glancing lazily at Mrs Timloe's grasping hands, which were rapidly losing, by this action, all blood required. "Therefore, those who wish to unseat this man we have chosen will have to contact him themselves. It will not be done through me." Now Mrs Chester opened her stance beyond Mrs Timloe, to address the table at large.

"Let me tell those assembled that this year's honoree is not simply a painter who explores. Of course the founders of this award must realize the limitations that these categories enforced. Perhaps we might also have looked only at short men with neat mustachios, as Mr Timloe was that as well. Yet this year, and finally, I might add, the man we have chosen is an artist. A true artist. He does not do anything so prosaic as merely painting this and that." Mrs Chester was gesturing sardonically with her hands as if she were painting, Mrs Wallace imagined, this and that. It was clear to Mrs Wallace that Mrs Chester intended to win the day, and public opinion, by persistent humiliation of her opponent. "Would Mr Timloe have preferred that? That is what you have long said. Do you believe that? This man hacks through the snarled underbrush of the past with machete before him. He does not have a mustache, I am sorry to say. He does not use a straw with orange juice. He is not rabid about his morning evacuations. He does not shout at the cook to quit banging pots while he is about them. We are not trying to exhume the namesake of this award, after all. Our artist need not wear sneakers while he swims in lakes so as to avoid leeches on his sensitive feet. So why must he dirty his clothes with paint and brush?"

To this Mrs Timloe, the widow of the man discussed, slapped the table with her purse, then put her aged knuckles before her to raise herself up—Mrs Wallace noticed how she wobbled upon the enormous cocktail rings there—and said, in a thin, elderly voice, which, though it had lost a certain measure of its pleasing timbre, still could muster volume when called upon to do so, "Mr Timloe was first a painter! First a painter! Second, he was an adventurer. Third, he was a lover! Speaking of such things as I told you in confidence about straws, evacuation and leeches is done only to discredit myself as an aged person. It is in this way that you try to silence my opinion. I will not be discredited, Mrs Chester. Not here and not by you."

"Of course it has been for a painter; all along it has been for a painter," said Mrs Chester without a trace of modulation or capitulation, and staring directly at the ancient woman before her, forty years her senior, whose long fingers seemed very heavy under the weight of her rings, and who eyed Mrs Chester with a tilted head; her affect suggested nothing so much to Mrs Wallace as a particularly angry bird who is plotting the most direct course between his beak and one's eyes. "But those categories no longer matter. You may prefer mediocrity but your son does not, and mediocrity will not be our selection." Mrs Chester waited to see, Mrs Wallace supposed, if Mrs Timloe would now take some time to defend mediocrity.

Mrs Chester looked around pointedly, skipping only Mrs Wallace with her imperious eyes. Mrs Wallace could see that Mrs Chester wished to shame away further comment, and she thought very little of her for it, for one could not think one's argument very strong if one could not stand to hear the opposition speak. To the end that Mrs Wallace had ascribed to her, Mrs Chester rapped twice with knuckles upon the table, and stared now at the Timloe widow with great intensity. "Here! If you still prefer a painter, I will show you whom else we might have selected." And she extracted several large reproductions from the largest of her folders.

Mrs Wallace did not see them head on, but they seemed to be of some subject medical, enlarged to painful degree as if they might soon be used in some enormous lecture hall for visual aids, when those normally sized would not suffice. They were so perfectly realistic as to have lost none of their deformity to artifice, and could only have been more disturbing if the tumorous hearts depicted did pump blood there, and leak from the canvas, uncontained by those few dimensions, and flinch when the proffered finger of an art enthusiast checked to see if they were real. Mrs Chester passed them around quite blithely, making sure the Timloe widow did not miss one of the prints.

But the Timloe widow, teetering there upon her rings, was not so easily dissuaded as Larinda, Mrs Wallace was encouraged to see—Mrs Wallace felt sure Larinda would fare better in all things if she did not cower so—and she drew up her voice, "Mr Timloe, in heaven, is saddened by this display. Believe me, Mrs Chester, he is saddened." The president too seemed saddened, and he looked curiously at Mrs Chester, who herself manifested no measure of that emotion. Mrs Wallace could say without doubt that the rest of the board seemed saddened as well.

Mrs Timloe sat back down, and was now taking some time with an inhaler. Mrs Wallace—who had been glad to see Mrs Timloe counter all that Mrs Chester presented, standing to the personal attack on her husband as she had, and flinchless as she had been at the gore-streaked pictures—now saw that she had been premature in believing that Mrs Timloe might go on with this indefinitely. Mrs Wallace felt sure that in her prime Mrs Timloe had disarmed any man who approached, but looking now upon her thin arms, Mrs Wallace felt equally sure that her body was no longer up to it, and at best she could be expected to seize hold of that man's weapon and cling there until, inevitably, her breath gave out, and she was shaken off into her nurse's arms.

After not a short time, Mrs Timloe spoke again from out of the side of her mouth unoccupied by the inhaler, "I will be ashamed, absolutely ashamed, to show my face at your event. And I won't do it then, and you shall have to explain that!"

But Mrs Chester continued, unperturbed, to the table at large. "Our artist is truly modern; he is a man of the modern world." And she took out from another of her files a series of prints which she passed around.

When they arrived at Mrs Timloe, she again hit the table with her purse. "If this is what the modern world offers," said the widow Timloe, with what Mrs Wallace was sure was the last measure of natural breath available to her within that hour, "I say that your millennium, and you yourself, are ridiculous!" and that was the last she said at the meeting.

Some there, Mrs Wallace noticed, seemed to interpret that to mean—and they were thankful of the release this interpretation allowed—that the widow Timloe had relented, and though she might bear this war home, she would no longer fight it at this table. Mrs Wallace could see clearly that she had not relented; she was simply much too old to stand against Mrs Chester.

Several cookies were now given medicinally to Mrs Timloe for her blood sugar, and her nurse escorted her out of the room. Mrs Wallace was sorry to see them go; besides herself, no one remained within that room who might be called upon to oppose that woman there.

The meeting sank into a torpor, save the vigorous Mrs Chester and her few allies from the Timloe committee, and it would take several minutes for the board members to regain themselves. They did so by pinching themselves and drinking water, and one or two even left the room and went Mrs Wallace knew not where, for they failed to return until the very end of the meeting. Mrs Wallace was sure they had suffered Mrs Chester's action with great pique, yet they had not the nerve to speak out.

The members of the board had not yet finished regaining themselves when Larinda, who had the last presentation of the committee chairs, began to speak. She did not take the time to make sure people were listening—Mrs Wallace felt sure that Larinda had to know one ought not wait for the impossible—and simply launched in. "I would like to begin," she said, "with a simple request for dignity on the part of my charity case." Mrs Wallace sighed, for Larinda often did not have control over the inadvertent meaning of her words, and was quite gifted at things like apologizing to people and insulting them all over again with the same meager collection.

"As of this year, the recipient of the Clark Stipend, to whom we have always referred as 'the poet in need,' must no longer be referred to as that. I am as guilty as the next, but I am very much ashamed, as must you all be. The winner of last year's stipend has informed me that he found the title quite dehumanizing, and did not like it when he was introduced that way. He informed me that when he visited the club, even the bartender would ask him, 'Would the poet in need like another scotch and soda?'" Larinda had found her last poet very touchy about the whole thing, Mrs Wallace remembered, which was perhaps the reason there was not competition for the chair; the poets one worked with were always extremely touchy.

"Of course, it is clear we must remind ourselves, he is selected as much for his work as for his need," Larinda continued, and then she cleared her throat. "The runner-up this year was perhaps a little needier, for he had a glass eye, but talent won out. One must, of course, choose the better poet. The winner is only a little less needy, but a great deal more qualified. So you see, we balance our selection." In fact, Larinda had wanted to pick the poet with the glass eye, though he wrote exceptionally bad doggerel, and had been almost about to send him his letter before Mrs Wallace stepped in. One could not simply give the money to the man with the least organic parts to his body. Then what

was being contested? Mrs Wallace, though she was not a member of the committee, had said this to Larinda in no uncertain terms, and finally Larinda had relented. After all, what did the poet with the glass eye need? He had not even said he needed a new glass eye, only that he had one already.

"Our poet's name is Arthur Chessler, and I will pass around his chapbook for you to look at. He needs several teeth pulled and is on the verge of an eviction." Larinda passed around the chapbooks, one going in each direction, as well as a copy of his dental x-rays.

"Do we have any other business?" the president asked sadly, holding the x-rays to the light as he said so, for Larinda's presentation had not helped diffuse the melancholy Mrs Chester had first created; even Mrs Wallace felt it, though she would not say it to her friend.

No one answered.

"I am very sorry about the way Mrs Chester attempted to murder that widow," said Larinda as they left the building. "Though she did, in the end, get her breath back, I was not absolutely sure that she would." And Mrs Wallace had to agree. Mrs Chester had made a most distressing meeting all around.

A man Mrs Wallace did not know well, who always sat at the end of the board table with his unlit pipe, waiting for the meeting to be over, made this same point as they exited the building. He stood there with lit match in hand: "I would not like to be under her sway," said the man. "I imagine not many have the strength to resist her."

"That cannot be true," said Mrs Wallace, though of course it was.

"My wife tells me that Mrs Chester has taken on a permanent houseguest. I fear for how she must be menacing him. She is likely to march into the guest bathroom and poison his water glass if he only disagrees with her about politics during dinner. Certainly she is capable. Perhaps we ought to take up a collection to free him," he said, and laughed, clearly at peace now that his pipe was lit.

"Who is that house guest?" Larinda asked, for never could she conceal her interest—though perhaps Mrs Wallace might wish her to ask, yet not so eagerly.

"A young man. A Henry Spector. His mother was once a member of this very club. It is such a shame to see the way the young men are now at such mercy all the time. Certainly they needed their own war."

Mrs Wallace did not reply to that.

She was more than a little put out. One did not like to hear that the loyalty of one's old friends was so tenuously held. Henry Spector's mother was a very old friend, and ought to have thought of her before Mrs Chester.

And yet, Mrs Wallace had been thinking most intently of her daughter's icy prospects; here clearly the other faucet had been turned, for Henry Spector, if memory served, had once been quite enormously worthwhile.

"He's been there for several days already," said the man eagerly. "One can go three weeks without food, but only three days without water," he said, and laughed. "Beyond that, eventually one needs renewed contact with human kindness."

At this Larinda laughed, and laid her hand on his arm, but Mrs Wallace, who would not allow herself a public comment upon the topic of Mrs Chester, held her unwilling tongue.

But on that other topic, of this young man who had just arrived, she and Larinda were not at all silent on the walk home. There was no reason they could divine that Katherine ought not to make a new friend, though she was still in possession of an old. ❧

SUBWAY
SKETCHBOOK

BY AGIR

WHY WE OCCUPY

LIBERTY PLAZA 2011
INTERVIEWS BY OLIVIA SCHANZER

There was something else my mother did that I've always remembered: "Always look for the helpers," she'd tell me. "There's always someone who is trying to help." I did, and I came to see that the world is full of doctors and nurses, police and firemen, volunteers, neighbors, and friends who are ready to jump in to help when things go wrong.

—Fred Rogers

Throughout his life, Mr. Rogers advised children who were worried about difficult and dangerous things they'd seen in the flesh or in the media to "look for the helpers." Wherever there is an accident, war or incident, there are people tending to others and ushering them to safe places, bandaging and hydrating and seeing to the comfort of those who are injured or in difficulty.

The following interviews are with Occupy Wall Street medics. Most days in the park, there were just as many people conducting interviews as sitting for them. And many of the participants in the occupation saw giving interviews as part of what they were doing there. But neither Shon nor Red wanted to be interviewed particularly. They were both somewhat reticent, at first, with a stranger, and were in no way looking for appreciation or acknowledgement for what they were doing. They humored me only because their friend in Comfort passed me on to them, and because I waylaid them by the medical tent where there wasn't an easy exit.

In 2012, during Occupy Sandy, I drove by Shon on a street in blacked-out Coney Island. A year later, he was still wearing a street-medic armband and seeing to people's needs.

Reading this five years later, my own enthusiasm hurts a little. If you can, take it, and consider the possibilities.

Red

I'M a street medic. When I'm here, I man the clinic between two and eight in the morning. Also, I kind of just do whatever needs to get done. I've been here for a while, so I can give a certain level of direction to people who are new.

As the clinic and the street medics separate, I've been doing less on the clinical side, leaving that to the trained nurses and doctors. I just do street-medic-related things. You know, bandaging people up after actions, before actions, during actions, and small stuff when they're around the camp. Around here, it's a lot more general-well-being-type things. Like, during the storm the other night, I was running around knocking on tent doors, making sure no one was freezing to death inside their tent.

Christine told me twenty-four people had hypothermia.

Might be a little low. People weren't prepared. It was nasty out here. It would have been a lot worse if we hadn't been running around all night, because barely any of those people actually came here and said, "I need help." Most of them were shivering their asses off, or couldn't walk. They were just sitting there, wherever they were.

What do you do for that? Do they have to go to the hospital?

If it's really bad. We sent one or two people to the hospital. Most of them we just warmed up. We had space heaters in our tents, and we just nursed them back to health. Yeah, that was one hell of a night.

Was that before they took away the generators?

No, that was not. We didn't have any generators. We had a propane space heater, and that was it.

Did you ever get them back?

Nah.

Do you think you'll ever get them back?

Well, we had a biodiesel generator. They took our generators because they said it was a combustion risk— it was a fire hazard—but the biofuel generator isn't a fire hazard. We were working on using that to create an electrical grid for the entire park. That plan is still moving forward once we get that back. We have the lawyers working on that, because there's no real reason for them to take that from us.

They are right in a certain respect, that having generators in this park isn't necessarily the best idea if there's a way to avoid it.

Tell me about how you became a medic.

Well, there was this action that happened in Union Square. It was the first time we got real press. I don't know if you remember the picture on the cover of the Daily News of that girl screaming after being maced? Right when that went down, I was working in Food. There were two medics, and that bench there was just a pile of medical supplies. There was no real order to it.

That was early on?

That was pretty early. I think it was, like, the second week. Food had everything down pretty well, and I just walked over and was like, "Hey, do you guys need help?" And they were like, "Yeah, we need help." Since then, I've gotten a plethora of street medic trainings, and have become someone who can actually contribute.

Have they been training you in here?

We've been reaching out to a lot of groups—street medic groups—and having people come from all over the country to do training.

What does the training consist of?

We did a seven-hour basic street medic training in the old J. P. Morgan Chase building at Twenty-Three Wall. We did eye-flush trainings for mace and pepper spray. We did a basic first aid one. We did an herbalist one. We did a Narcan overdose training. A.E.D./C.P.R. training.

What is Narcan?

Narcan is the drug you administer to someone who has overdosed on opiates.

Have you been called to a lot of things?

Yeah. I mean, it varies depending on what's going on that day. Some days it's a lot of hand injuries from drumming. [Laughs.] Some days, you just get guy after guy coming in with their hands all bloody, like, "I need to go back out and play!" Other days, after a brutal action or something, they'll come back with sprained ankles, they got hit, they got maced, stuff like that. Most of the time, especially at night, we stay pretty busy, but what that is depends on the environment for the day.

You said you're working the overnight?

Yeah. When I'm here, I work the overnight.

Are you able to sleep?

If I'm here, I'll sleep. I'll work during the day, then I'll do an overnight shift, and sleep the next day. But if it's really bad . . . I went three days without sleep, like, a week ago. Sometimes things just keep coming up, and unless you want to feel like a terrible person in the morning, you can't just be like, "All right, I'm going to sleep!"

It's kind of like in a hospital.

Yeah, something like that.

How did you originally get into the movement?

How I originally got here? People have been asking me that a lot. I'm not entirely sure . . . something having to do with the Internet, I guess. I found it somewhere on the Internet. Then it started up, and I watched the LiveStream when I was at the job I used to have. I'm like, "Man, this is great! I never thought something like this would happen! I need to go down there! I need to go down there!" And a couple days in, I finally just said, "Fuck it!" I took a couple days off work and came down, and haven't been able to leave since.

Are you from New York?

Yeah, I'm from upstate New York. I used to live down here, but it was too cutthroat for me.

I hear that. Tell me about how you quit your job.

So I took two days off work and I came down here. I took a bus, and then a train. I came down, I spent the day here, and I slept here. Woke up the next day, did it again. Around Saturday or Sunday, I realized I can't leave. I just ... I don't think I'm physically capable of doing it.

I've been bitching about the state of the world and the state of this country for years. I never thought something like this would happen. Part of what I was bitching about was how my generation were too content with their Xboxes and their reality T.V. shows to ever get up and try to change things. And then they did. I couldn't pass that up; it was such a large part of my philosophy on why things have declined.

That's funny because I used to bitch about your generation, too. Now I'm eating my words.

Give it a little while. [Laughs.]

I'm impressed, though. They did get a bad rap.

[Laughs.] Deservedly so.

I'm an Xer and we didn't do shit, so I can't criticize you guys. We didn't have Xboxes, but we didn't do shit, either.

ᢒ

Did you know people who were down here?

Not when I first got here, but I made friends really quick. It was a lot smaller when I started coming. Most of the people I know now—we've all been here since either the beginning or right near the beginning. Then, it was much more like everyone was here for the same reason. Everyone was here to try to make this work. There was a lot less people just here to party, just here to hang out. We were all busting our asses working ridiculous hours, and we got to know each other and became good friends. So now I know plenty of people here. ᢒ

Shon

I'M part of the Medical crew here at Zuccotti Square. Street medics. We basically provide medical support for the occupation, for the different marches and demonstrations that are in line with the broader scope of the occupation, and for the ninety-nine percent.

You go along on the marches with your equipment?

Yeah. We're there to treat anything from blisters to pepper spray to baton wounds. We do jail support; when people get out of jail, we're there to provide medical support in case they have any injuries.

In addition to pepper spray and baton wounds, what other kinds of things happen on the marches?

A lot of cough drops being handed out. We keep people hydrated. If they don't bring their own water, we try to have water for them. We've also been able—in some cases, like on the Brooklyn Bridge—to negotiate with the police about providing emergency medical attention. We've been able to get some people out of being arrested.

Are the street medics also active in the park?

Yeah, the street medics do rounds. If there's somebody that needs medical attention, we'll go find them and assess them. We see if they can be treated there on the spot. They might need to come to our clinic here, or they might be rushed to the emergency room.

Have you sent a lot of people to the emergency room?

There's been quite a few, yeah.

I've heard some horror stories about the big snowstorm, and the number of people who had hypothermia.

There were a lot of cases of different stages of hypothermia, but it's a hard number to count. There were wet and shivering people that felt like they didn't need any medical attention. A lot of them did self-care—went to Comfort, got new clothes, dried out, went to a restaurant or something—and got to feeling better. That night, it was easier to count those who didn't show signs or symptoms than those who did.

Were you a medic before the occupation?

A little experience in street medic work, but this is a new type of experience, the occupation. The ongoing occupation is something new in the medical field.

How'd you get involved in doing it?

I found out there was no organized street medic presence here. I did want to come down and help out and be a part of it, but when I found out there was no street medic crew, I came down to help with that.

When I got here there was medics, but most of them had to leave. So then we made a call out to the General Assembly for anybody that had medical experience.

Were there a lot of people who had experience?

I think that night we got seven. We started out with, I think, two trash bags full of supplies, and we put our own personal funds together and got other stuff we needed. We had some donations coming in, and it just started growing and growing. Now we're at the point where we have a really well-operated medical clinic here, with doctors and nurses on staff. We have emotional support and alternative health. Our crew's gotten a lot bigger, and we've evolved immensely.

How many street medics do you have?

It's hard to tell. Right now, I think we have on-site . . . there's four right now. We've got maybe around twenty that have their own schedules and can be here when they can.

How many doctors and nurses would you say you have?

We probably have four doctors, and somewhere between six and eight nurses. We also have other-skill-level people working in the clinic.

And where are those guys coming from? The city?

All over.

Can you talk about why you decided to get involved?

To participate in direct democracy. This is a wonderful chance to experience it and watch it grow, and to work out all the things that come up. We're constantly facing new walls in front of us. We find positive ways to take down those barriers, and to make different pathways from what we experience in our normal lives. That alone is priceless. To be able to have this opportunity in direct democracy is a beautiful thing.

Had you been an activist before this?

Yeah.

What kinds of things were you involved in?

Day-to-day community activism: social justice issues, human rights issues, free food programs.

In New York?

Philadelphia.

Like, soup kitchen kind of thing?

Food Not Bombs. Free food distros.

Have you been involved with food distribution here?

No. I love doing food, and I love sweeping and sanitation, but my calling here is Medic. I haven't done anything else here. [Laughs.]

It seems like a lot of people find a new calling here.
Anything else that you'd like to put on the record?

I think one thing is important: What we've learned from this, we can take to our own communities. I would love to see direct democracy in the form of General Assemblies and Spokes Councils in every neighborhood. That would allow us to work on the issues that directly impact where we live, and directly impact our neighbors.

The Spokes Council just started up, didn't it?

Yep. I think tomorrow's the first one.

Can you explain to me how it works?

All working groups go.

The whole working group goes?

If they're able to. You know, we have to have people on shift here. *They* won't be able to go, but the whole working group that's able to goes. One person is the representative, and it rotates; there's not only one representative. The representative, at any time during the meeting, can be switched out. So it's not a matter of authority, or any leadership taking on that role. It's just a spokesperson, speaking to represent the group, and they'll be with their working group.

So what kind of issues is the Spokes Council going to handle, as opposed to just General Assembly?

Logistics of this park, I believe. What's going on here, things we're working on. Medics will be talking about self care, winterization, other things that have been going on. We'll be able to speak at the Spokes Council about those issues, and address those to the other working groups and caucuses here, which I'm really excited for.

The General Assembly, from what I understand, will be working on issues—the movement as a whole, nationally or globally. Personally, I haven't been able to sit in a whole General Assembly for a long time. I'm glad that I'll be able to participate again, to have the time to talk about the issues and things that we're working on. A lot of working groups—they just meet on their own, work out their own issues, and try to send somebody to the General Assembly to do a report-back. It wasn't effective. So I'm excited for the Spokes Council.

I'd heard, also, that some people who were not in the spirit of General Assembly were shouting.

Oh, yeah, since the beginning. People thought that was their opportunity to get up and say why they're here, and list off all the things that are wrong in the world. The General Assembly had set up what they call the People's Soapbox at the end of the General Assembly to give them time to do that. A lot of people are new to the process. They're really hyped and have a lot to say.

There are some disruptions, and there will be, but the facilitators, especially, are working really hard to correct that, to make the meetings go smoother so more can get done.

Is the Spokes Council closed to the general population here?

No. They can either join a working group, which everybody is encouraged to do, or there's the Occupiers Working Group. People that live here can join the Spokes Council as an Occupier. I think that's great. That addressed a lot of concerns that it was closed.

But I encourage everybody to join a working group. It's a very productive way to plug in to what's going on, have something to do, and help out. We do need a lot of help here. There was just a call for help from the kitchen, to do lunch.

Just today?

Just a few minutes ago. And Sanitation always needs help, I know. There's stuff that has to get done.

I know some people are bothered by the people who are not working and not helping out. Where do you stand on that?

I would like to talk to the people, and find out what are some of their concerns with working groups that they might have an interest in joining. I've talked to some people, and they wanted to join some type of working group, but they felt, for whatever reason, it wasn't a good place for them to be. So I encouraged them to start their own. We really haven't made it clear that there is that avenue, too.

What kind of working groups need to be made that aren't there?

I would like to see a group of people who were homeless in New York City before the occupation started. Let them have the opportunity to put their heads together and see what they can come up with. Some of their ideas could make this occupation better. ℯ

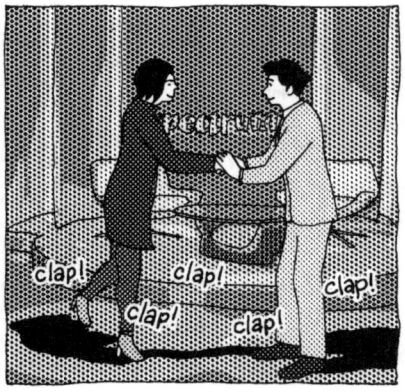